WORLD OF ENGINEERING

BUILDING A SKYSCRAPER

NATALIE HUMPHREY

PowerKiDS press

Published in 2024 by The Rosen Publishing Group, Inc.
2544 Clinton Street, Buffalo, NY 14224

Portions of this work were originally authored by Therese Shea and published as *How a Skyscraper Is Built.* All new material in this edition was authored by Natalie Humphrey.

Editor: Natalie Humphrey
Designer: Rachel Rising

Photo Credits: Cover, ST-art/Shutterstock.com; Cover, pp. 1-24 Alef-Beth/Shutterstock.com; Cover, pp. 1-24 Artistdesign29/Shutterstock.com; Cover, pp. 1, 3, 22-24 RoseRodionova/Shutterstock.com; Cover, p.1 Creative Hawk/Shutterstock.com; p. 5 Tavarius/Shutterstock.com; p. 6 Another77/Shutterstock.com; p. 7 Vadim Ratnikov/Shutterstock.com; p. 9 kckate16/Shutterstock.com; p. 11 Red ivory/Shutterstock.com; p. 13 narai chal/Shutterstock.com; p. 15 Dmitry Kalinovsky/Shutterstock.com; p. 16 Albo/Shutterstock.com; p. 17 IrinaK/Shutterstock.com; p. 19 shigemi okano/Shutterstock.com; p. 20 zuperia/Shutterstock.com; p. 20 Angel_AMX/Shutterstock.com; p. 21 Macrovector/Shutterstock.com; p. 21 AmazeinDesign/Shutterstock.com; p. 21 rzarek/Shutterstock.com.

Author: Humphrey, Natalie.
Title: Building a skyscraper / Natalie Humphrey.
Description: Buffalo, New York : Powerkids Press, 2024. | Series: World of engineering | Includes index, glossary, and bibliographic information
Identifiers: ISBN 9781642826524 (pbk) | ISBN 9781642826531 (library bound) | ISBN 9781642826548 (ebook)
Subjects: LCSH: Architecture-- Juvenile literature | Engineering--Juvenile literature
Classification: LCC NA2555 H86 2024 | DDC 720--dc24

Manufactured in the United States of America

CPSIA Compliance Information: Batch #CSPK24. For Further Information contact Rosen Publishing at 1-800-237-9932.

CONTENTS

THE TALLEST BUILDINGS

What is a skyscraper? In 1880, skyscrapers were buildings that were between 10 and 20 stories tall. But today, many buildings are much taller. A skyscraper now is usually a building that's taller than 40 or 50 stories.

These giant buildings take a lot of work to keep them standing. After **architects** create the **design** for the skyscraper, engineers take over. It's up to the engineering team to oversee construction on the building. They make sure it's strong enough to stand against **gravity** and other forces.

ENGINEERING WONDERS

An engineer is a person who uses math and science to solve problems. Different kinds of engineers work to build a skyscraper.

AS OF 2010, THE TALLEST SKYSCRAPER IN THE WORLD IS BURJ KHALIFA IN THE CITY OF DUBAI IN THE UNITED ARAB EMIRATES. IT'S 2,717 FEET (828 M) TALL!

To build a skyscraper, engineers need to use certain materials, or something from which something else can be made. These materials need to be strong enough to hold the weight of the skyscraper. Two key materials used in skyscrapers are steel and reinforced concrete.

Steel is made out of iron and the element carbon. Reinforced concrete is a mix of **cement**, water, and gravel or sand. This mixture is poured onto steel rods. With steel and reinforced concrete, workers can build skyscrapers that won't fall over.

ENGINEERING WONDERS

Workers use many other materials to build skyscrapers. Some skyscrapers may also use glass; metals such as aluminum and stainless steel; and rock such as granite, marble, and limestone.

BUILDERS OFTEN USE REINFORCED CONCRETE TO CREATE THE FLOOR AND **COLUMNS** IN SKYSCRAPERS.

BUILDING A STRONG FOUNDATION

All skyscrapers start with a strong **foundation**. To create a foundation, workers dig a pit deep down into the **bedrock**. They then blast holes into the bedrock, and place steel or reinforced concrete support columns into the holes.

If the bedrock is too deep to reach, workers can drive columns called piles into the soil until they've reached the bedrock. In another method, they can drill **shafts** into the soil and bedrock and place steel rods in them. Pouring concrete inside the shafts makes them strong.

ENGINEERING WONDERS

To help the skyscraper's foundation hold more weight, engineers use spread footing. This means the bottom of the skyscraper's **vertical** columns are wider than the top. This allows them to carry more weight.

THE TALLER THE BUILDING, THE STRONGER THE FOUNDATION NEEDS TO BE!

THE SUPERSTRUCTURE

Just like humans, skyscrapers need skeletons too! In humans, a skeleton is the strong frame of bones that supports the body. A skyscraper's skeleton, also called a superstructure, helps to keep it standing tall while gravity pulls down on it. After building the foundation, engineers begin working on the superstructure.

Vertical and **horizontal** columns are joined to form the superstructure of a skyscraper. There may also be **diagonal** beams. Steel usually forms the superstructure.

ENGINEERING WONDERS

At the center, or core, of many skyscrapers is concrete. This helps carry some of the weight of the building.

WORKERS USE HUGE CRANES TO HELP BUILD THE SKYSCRAPER.

While many skyscrapers may look like they're made of glass, they really aren't! Their superstructures are doing the hard work of holding the building up, so the outside walls can be made of anything. This includes glass or metal.

As a skyscraper's superstructure is built higher and higher, crews begin to work to lay floors and finish construction on lower stories. This work includes adding electrical wires to power the building, bathrooms, inner walls, and heating and cooling.

ENGINEERING WONDERS

To keep people on higher floors safe in case of a fire, builders put in fireproof materials and sprinkler systems.

ENGINEERS REGULARLY CHECK THE SPRINKLER SYSTEMS IN SKYSCRAPERS TO MAKE SURE THEY'RE WORKING RIGHT.

GOING UP

Elevators are an important part of a skyscraper. Without elevators, people would need to walk up hundreds of stairs. Most skyscrapers feature an elevator shaft in the middle of the building, but some elevators are on an outside wall.

The taller a building is, the more people occupy it. That means more elevators are needed. Engineers use math to figure out how many elevators are needed to keep people moving. They also figure out how each elevator will affect the skyscraper's structure.

ENGINEERING WONDERS

Some elevators are designed to carry people up and down. Other elevators, called freight elevators, are designed to carry heavier materials. Some skyscrapers have both elevators!

WORKERS BUILT THE FIRST ELEVATOR TO CARRY PEOPLE IN A BUILDING IN NEW YORK CITY IN 1857.

STANDING UP TO NATURE

Engineers need to consider wind when building a skyscraper. Taller buildings may move back and forth in the wind. This doesn't feel safe to the people inside, even if the building is strong enough to hold up in the wind. Engineers construct skyscrapers in certain ways to help.

In shorter skyscrapers, tightened connections between horizontal and vertical beams can keep the building from moving in the wind. Taller skyscrapers use stronger cores to keep the building from swaying. Some tall skyscrapers may even have more than one core!

ENGINEERING WONDERS

The Empire State Building and the Chrysler Building, both skyscrapers in New York City, use reinforced steel and diagonal beams to stop them from moving in the wind.

IF WINDS ARE STRONG ENOUGH, THEY CAN STILL CAUSE DAMAGE TO THE SKYSCRAPER.

In some places, engineers worry about more than just gravity and wind. Some skyscrapers must be safe from natural **disasters** such as **earthquakes**. Skyscrapers built in places where earthquakes are common are made of materials that won't break when the quake starts.

Some earthquake-proof buildings use a foundation that moves with the earthquake instead of the building. Other skyscrapers use a weight to move in the opposite direction as the earthquake. Engineers use these and other ways to keep buildings standing during earthquakes.

ENGINEERING WONDERS

Skyscrapers are an important part of city planning today. The taller the skyscrapers are, the more people can live and work inside!

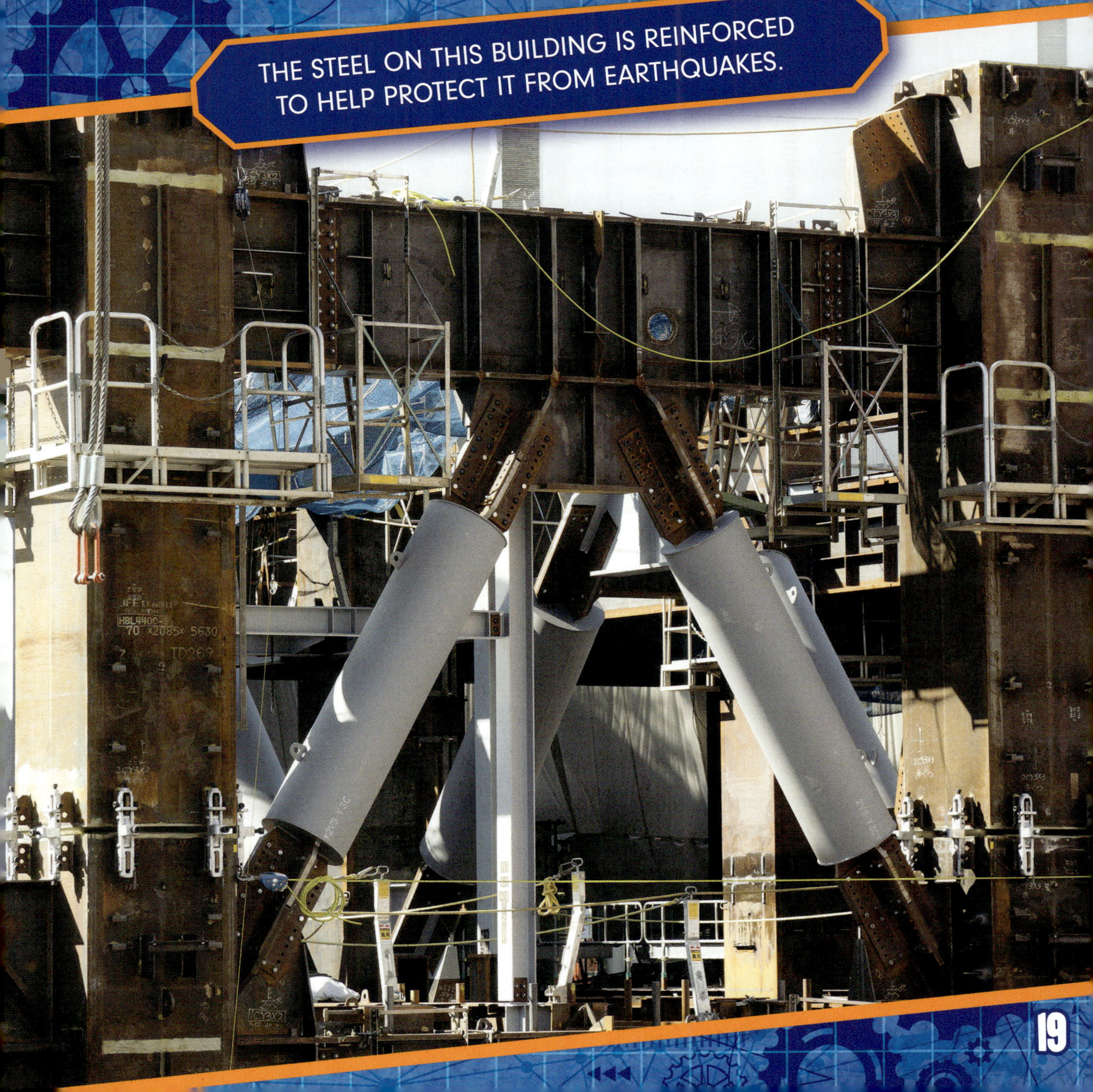

THE STEEL ON THIS BUILDING IS REINFORCED TO HELP PROTECT IT FROM EARTHQUAKES.

MAKE YOUR OWN SKYSCRAPER

Now that you know how engineers build skyscrapers, it's time to build your own!

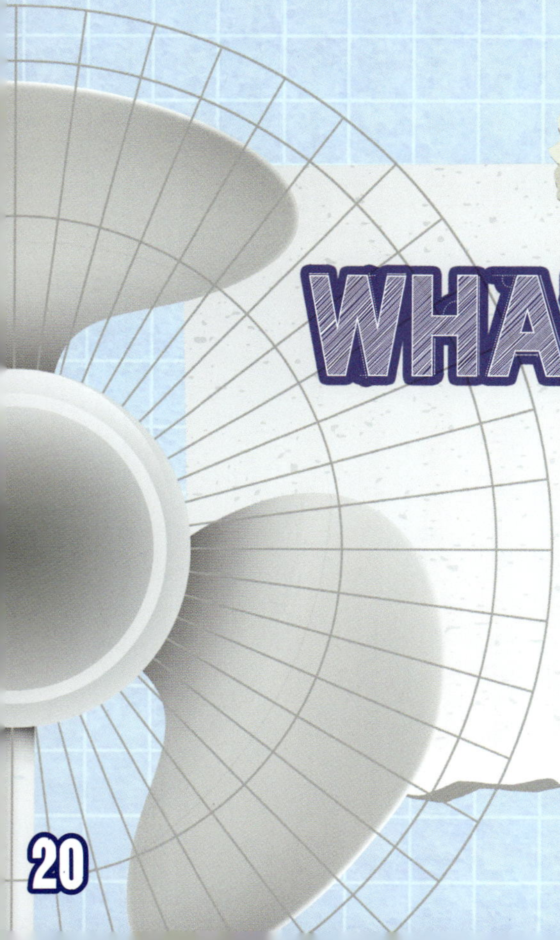

WHAT YOU NEED

- fan
- newspaper
- scissors
- tape

HOW TO

1. Roll the newspaper into a tube.
2. Tape the newspaper tube vertically.
3. Roll a few more newspaper rolls to make foundation tubes.
4. Secure the foundation tubes to the ground.
5. Tape the foundation tubes to the vertical tube.
6. Test how strong your structure is with the fan.
7. If your structure falls over, try building a stronger foundation!

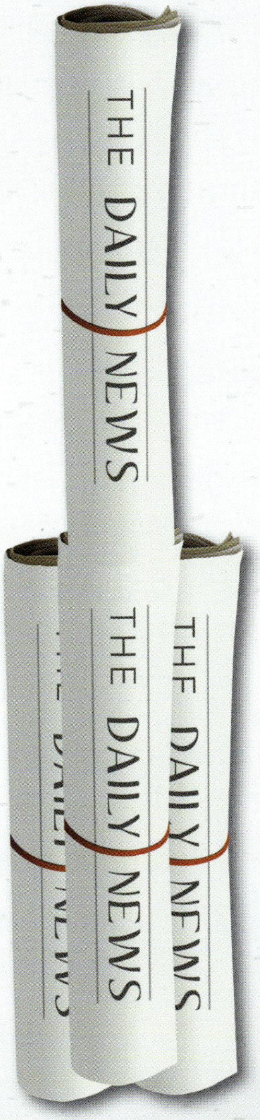

GLOSSARY

architect: A person who designs buildings.

bedrock: The solid rock that lies under the surface of the ground.

cement: A soft gray powder mixed with water and other substances to make concrete.

column: A tall, strong supporting post.

design: To create a plan for something. Also, the plan itself.

diagonal: Slanting from one side to another.

disaster: Something that happens suddenly and causes much suffering and loss for many people.

earthquake: A shaking of the ground caused by the movement of Earth's crust.

foundation: A structure, usually made of stone or concrete, that supports a building from underneath.

gravity: The force that pulls objects toward Earth's center.

horizontal: Level with the line that seems to form where the earth meets the sky.

shaft: A tunnel dug deep into the ground.

verical: Positioned up and down.

FOR MORE INFORMATION

BOOKS

Amin, Anita Nahta. *Amazing Skyscrapers.* Minneappolis, MN: Pogo Books, 2023.

Bowman, Chris. *Skyscrapers.* Minneapolis, MN: Bellwether Media, 2019.

Newland, Sonya. *Extraordinary Skyscrapers: The Science of How and Why They Were Built.* North Mankato, MN: Capstone Press, 2019.

WEBSITES

Building Big
www.pbs.org/wgbh/buildingbig/skyscraper/basics.html
Learn more about different styles of architecture and skyscrapers throughout history.

National Geographic Kids
kids.nationalgeographic.com/awesome-8/article/skyscrapers
Check out more skyscrapers from around the world.

Publisher's note to educators and parents: Our editors have carefully reviewed these websites to ensure that they are suitable for students. Many websites change frequently, however, and we cannot guarantee that a site's future contents will continue to meet our high standards of quality and educational value. Be advised that students should be closely supervised whenever they access the internet.

INDEX